ILLUSTRATED
WALKS AND DRIVES
in the
NORTH YORK MOORS
A Pitkin Guide

INTRODUCTION

The North York National Park covers an area of 553 square miles (1432 sq km). Predominantly, this is a region of high heather moorland into which deep, narrow dales have been carved, but there is drama, too, at the fringes. To the east, the moors reach right up to the coast which falls away in tall cliffs; while, to the west and north, the land rears up in a steep escarpment that stands high above the surrounding plain. The land was formed over the long aeons of geological time. The bedrock was created some 150 million years ago when the area was covered by shallow seas. Then, about eighty million years ago, forces within the Earth heaved this great mass up to create 'the Cleveland Dome'. It was to sink and rise again, and be eaten away and eroded by the sea and the natural forces of wind and water. In the ice age, the ice blocked the natural flow of water and the dales were flooded. Great lakes formed and, where the lake in what is now Eskdale overflowed, the waters raced down to the lake at Pickering carving out the deep, sinuous valley of Newtondale.

Humans, too, have played their part in creating the landscape we see today. Forest was cleared, and the sheep that graze the heather keep it clear, nibbling away at any young shoots that might try to establish themselves. Controlled burning ensures that young heather develops to provide food for sheep and for the red grouse. In recent times, woodland has returned in large areas in the form of conifer plantations. These dense patches of woodland make use of poor land which otherwise have little economic use, but they

A misty morning over the moors.

seldom have the visual appeal and variety that one finds in broad-leaved woodland.

Even though moorland is such a dominant feature in this landscape, walkers will find that it has great variety. At first glance, the great expanses of bracken and heather may seem bleak, almost featureless, but they are never deserted. The air echoes with the calls of birds, from the rather plaintive 'pee-wit' cry of the lapwing to the harsher, unwelcoming 'go-back, go-back' of the red grouse. The grouse are the reason for a feature of the moors — the lines of butts, where the guns wait as the autumn shooting season begins. The valleys have a very different character, softer, often heavily wooded, and dotted with the traditional building of the region, stone built with pantile roofs. Add to that a splendid and often wild coastline, where little villages squeeze into narrow valleys and you have a region with no shortage of delights to meet every taste.

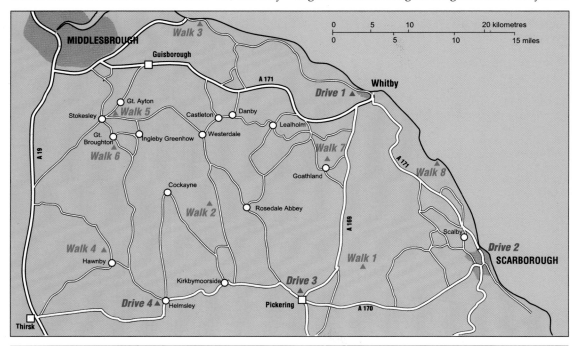

THE WALKS

The walks included in this book have been devised with family outings in mind. Even if you are inexperienced, however, this should not mean that you can be careless or thoughtless. You need to plan your day in advance. First read the walk account and become familiar with the route on good maps. Next, work out a rough schedule of walking, visits, rests and refreshments bearing in mind opening times. Equip yourself with the right kind of clothing and supplies.

Out on the ramble, keep your wits about you: field boundaries may have been moved, trees taken away, or new roads constructed. To give you some idea of what to expect, the walks have been graded. **Easy** walks take about two hours and are generally well signposted along made-up paths and tracks. **Moderate** walks take up to four hours or so; the terrain is mostly firm but there may be an occasional steep climb or rough track.

Walks are described as **difficult** either because of their length or because they do not always follow well-trodden and easily identified footpaths. They need careful planning, detailed maps, and the use of a compass. The North York Moors might seem to present fewer dangers than more mountainous districts, such as the Lake District or Snowdonia, but the high moors are very bare, offering no protection at all from bad weather, and, in mist or low cloud, can seem alarmingly featureless. But it is this very wildness that gives the region its unique character. It is there to be enjoyed and, with careful preparation, it can be enjoyed safely. The walks provide gentle introductions to the area as well as more demanding routes for the energetic. There is something here for everyone.

Countryside Care

The countryside lives and breathes. It is home for many, provides a living for some, and plays a vital role in our economy. It is also the basis of our natural heritage.

Those who walk in the countryside tread a tightrope: between access and conservation, involvement and interference, utilization and preservation. Organizations, such as the National Trust or National Park authorities, are dedicated to preserving our heritage by ensuring access to certain areas while at the same time planning for the future. Walkers enjoy the highlights of the countryside at their leisure, but they owe it to themselves and to others to conserve these pleasures for the generations to come. We have rights, but we also have responsibilities.

Rights of Way and Access

Public footpaths, tracks, and bridleways are 'public property' in the same sense as a road or car park. They are not owned by the public, however; the landowner, while retaining rights of ownership, 'dedicates' a path or road to public use so that a right of way is established.

A right of way means the public is permitted to cross land by the designated route, without straying from it or causing damage. If you leave the path you may be trespassing; if you leave litter, or damage fences or crops, you lay yourself open to legal action. A right of way remains as such until it is revoked ('extinguished') in law, by the local authority. It is irrelevant how often the route is used, or whether it is overgrown, or blocked by a locked gate or a heap of manure. In some cases, however, rights of way may be diverted to permit buildings, roadworks, or farming.

Footpaths and other public rights of way are indicated on the Ordnance Survey 1:50 000 (Landranger) series. In addition, public access is customary in common land because fencing it to keep people out is both legally complex and impractical.

Beware of the Bull

Complicated bye-laws govern the release of bulls into fields crossed by a right of way. It is best to assume that any bull is potentially dangerous and to take a detour or avoid it if possible.

What to wear

For all but the shortest routes, the walker should be properly clothed. Purpose-designed boots and a waterproof top are not only sensible for comfort and safety, they also help you enjoy to the full your day out. The first essential is some type of water- and wind-proof outer garment such as an anorak, cagoule, or coat, preferably with a hood. Modern lightweight, 'breathable' anoraks can be rolled and stowed away when not in use.

For warmth, the main requirement is several layers of insulating material such as woollen sweaters or thermofleece garments. These can be taken off as the weather improves, or added to if the wind

A wayside halt.

strengthens. Wool 'breathes' to minimize sweating yet retains body heat effectively. A warm shirt is also recommended.

Do not wear denim jeans for walking. They are usually too restrictive and have poor insulating qualities especially when wet. Walking trousers should be warm and comfortably loose to allow movement without chafing. On long walks, carry waterproof overtrousers.

Feet are the walker's best friends, so care for them. There are as many opinions about the best kind of footwear for walking as there are feet on the footpaths. Nowadays, there is a huge range of boots and walking shoes available and it is sensible to buy the best that you can afford. Good outdoor clothing suppliers can advise you or, better still, read the reviews in the outdoor magazines and then buy the boots that suit you best. Good ankle support is a must in rocky and difficult terrain. For short walks on easy ground a pair of tough, comfortable shoes may be adequate. Wellingtons may be suited to very wet ground but they quickly become uncomfortable and tend to rub up blisters. Whatever the footwear, thick woollen or loop-stitch socks are the sensible choice beneath; at a price, the so-called 'super-socks' are now available. Most footwear needs to be broken in and must fit comfortably before you take to the paths.

On longer walks it is wise to carry a few extras in your rucksack: a sweater, a spare pair of socks, a warm hat, and a pair of thermal gloves.

What to take

Certain items are basic to any respectable walk. A rucksack and good maps are vital. Other equipment depends on the nature of the walk and personal interests. The rucksack or backpack has many advantages over a hand-carried bag. With a rucksack you can take more, carry it more comfortably, and leave your hands free (an important safety consideration in rough terrain). There is an enormous variety of rucksacks available. For a half-day or day walk choose a medium-sized model of about 30 litres capacity, made of nylon or similar, that fits you snugly without chafing.

A selection of maps should always be at hand. Do not rely solely on the sketch maps in this book. These sketch maps are intended for use with Ordnance Survey maps (1:50 000 Landranger series or, better, the Outdoor Leisure Maps and Pathfinder maps at 1:25 000 — about 2½ inches to the mile).

A good map provides details of rights of way, viewpoints, parking, conveniences, and telephones, and lets you identify distant features. A compass is necessary for map-reading because paths are often indistinct or routes unmarked across open country. Local guidebooks and field guides point out items of interest as you go, rather than after you return.

On a long walk, carry extra food with you unless you are sure of a 'refuelling' stop. Concentrated high-energy food, such as chocolate or mintcake, revives flagging limbs and spirits, and a modern lightweight vacuum-flask provides a welcome hot beverage. A few sticking plasters, a penknife, and a length of string may come in handy so keep them in a side pocket in your rucksack. A modern 'blister-repair kit' can be a real boon.

Walking is an excellent way of reaching an unusual viewpoint or approaching wary wildlife. A camera records the scene and 'collects' nature without damaging it, and binoculars permit close-ups of animals about their business. Walk with these items at the ready — you never know when they might be needed.

The bridge over the River Rye, Hawnby.

Maps

A walker without a map is like a car without a steering wheel. It is essential to obtain good maps, learn how to read and interpret them, and check your route before you set off. Most experienced walkers use a combination of maps, as described below. The sketch maps in this book are not intended to be your sole guide: use them in combination with Ordnance Survey (OS) and other maps in guide books and local publications.

The OS maps come in two main scales. First is the Landranger 1:50 000 series (about 1¼ inches to the mile). These maps cover the entire country and show footpaths, bridleways, rights of way, farm buildings, and other features. They are useful for general planning and for gaining an overall impression of the area. To cover the North York Moors, including York itself, you will need sheet numbers 99, 100, 101, 105, and 106.

The second main OS scale is 1:25 000 (roughly 2½ inches to the mile). These maps are published as individual sheets of the First and Second Series —

covering the entire country, and as large fold-out Outdoor Leisure Maps for recreational areas, holiday regions, and national parks. The 1:25 000 maps are often called the 'walker's maps' because they show features important to walkers and ramblers, such as field boundaries, viewpoints, rescue posts, and rights of way. Up-to-date 1:25 000 maps are recommended for use with the maps in this book. The Outdoor Leisure Maps of the North York Moors National Park are numbers 26 (Western Area) and 27 (Eastern Area).

For driving, the OS Routemaster Series, at 1:250 000 (roughly 1 inch to 4 miles) is useful, and for this area you will need Sheet 5 (Northern England) and Sheet 6 (East Midlands and Yorkshire). Further information is available from the Ordnance Survey.

Another useful series is the Footpath Maps published by the Ramblers Association (RA). These are at

Captain Cook

If North Yorkshire can be said to have a hero, then it must be James Cook. Born in 1728, he began his career as an ordinary seaman and 'came up through the hawse-hole', the old naval term for one who rose through the ranks, to be appointed captain. He was one of the greatest of all English navigators. He established Australia as an island continent, circumnavigated Antarctica, and died at the hands of Hawaiian natives. He has not been forgotten in his native land. One relic you will not see, however, is the cottage where he was born, at least not in North Yorkshire. In 1934 it was taken to pieces and shipped to Melbourne. In return, stones from Point Hicks, where Cook first landed in Australia, were sent to England and built into an obelisk at Great Ayton (Drive 4). Cook spent much of his

childhood in the town, and the school he attended is now a museum devoted to his life, and he is also commemorated by a second, far grander, obelisk on a hill above the town.

Cook learned his seamanship on the north-east coast. He was apprenticed to a draper at Staithes, but showed more interest in the boats in the harbour than in cloth at the counter. He was soon apprenticed to his true trade of the sea in nearby Whitby. The home of his employer in Grape Lane is now a museum, and his statue looks out to sea from West Cliff. All four of his ships were built here, drawing on the experience gained in designing ships for the hazardous Arctic whaling trade. Looking at Whitby today, it is difficult to see it as home to ships that once travelled to the other side of the world.

The Cook monument, Great Ayton.

The North Yorkshire Moors Railway at Newton Dale.

1:25 000 scale and show many details such as footpaths, tracks, rides and bridleways, car parks and gates. For details of regions covered by these maps contact a local RA representative via a regional newspaper or community magazine, or enquire at the RA Head Office.

Safety

The routes described in this book can be completed safely by the average family provided basic safety rules are observed.

1. Wear suitable clothing and footwear, as described in the previous pages.
2. Always assume the weather may suddenly turn nasty. Carry an extra sweater and a waterproof, or even a small umbrella.
3. Obtain a good map and learn to read it. The maps in this book are intended for use in conjunction with detailed walkers' maps such as the Ordnance Survey 1:25 000 series.
4. On longer walks take some energy-giving food, such as chocolate or glucose lozenges, and a drink of some kind.
5. Allow plenty of time to complete your walk. A good average is 2 miles an hour — less if you enjoy views or watch nature at work.
6. If possible, have a first-aider in the group, and take change for emergency phone calls.

There is one over-riding rule that applies to all walking in wild country. If in any doubt at all, always err on the side of safety. There is no pleasure to be had from wandering lost on an empty moorland in a wet, chilling mist that has obliterated every landmark from view. The walk will still be there on another day — make sure that you are, too!

Transport on the Moors

No one can tell now which tracks were used for crossing the moors in prehistoric times, but the archaeological evidence provided by such sites as the round barrow known as Robin Hood's Butts and the remains of Bronze Age field systems tells us that people have lived on and around the moor for many thousands of years. One route, by tradition at least, was an important route in ancient times. Popularly known as 'Hambleton Street', the track runs for some 15 miles (24 km) from the Hambleton Hills to Sutton Bank, where it divides, one track heading off towards what is now York, the other towards Malton. Certainly, the number of prehistoric sites that line the route, part of which is now incorporated into the Cleveland Way National Trail, seem to support the theory. What is certain is that, in medieval times, this was part of the drove road along which cattle were herded en route from Scotland to markets as far away as London. But that is to move forward in time a little too quickly, for one of the most interesting of all the old transport routes in the whole region takes us back to Roman times.

The Romans had a set of four military camps at Cawthorn, just north of Pickering, and it was from here that they built a road heading off across Wheeldale Moor. Known as Wade's Causeway, there is a beautifully preserved section of this road near Goathland, which is visited during Walk 7. It follows the typical Roman pattern of first building a low embankment, known as an 'agger', on which large paving stones were laid to create the surface. This is still a remarkably fine roadway, the stones surviving after 2000 years of use, and it is interesting to see the care that went into details such as the little stone conduits that carried drainage water from the moor under the roadway.

The next major change that we can still detect today came with the arrival of monks and the establishment of their monasteries and abbeys, such as Rievaulx and Rosedale. Pilgrims were guided across the lonely moors by waymarks, much as modern walkers are on long-distance footpaths. The most famous of these is one of the Ralph crosses high on Westerdale Moor (Drive 4), set at a point where many ways meet — it is the official emblem of the National Park. The monks, however, needed roads for more than just visitors on pilgrimage. They brought sheep to graze the uplands, and grew wealthy on the fleeces, which needed to be taken to market. Pack horses carried the loads in panniers slung across their backs, and, to help them across some of the boggier valleys and up and down the steeper slopes, narrow stone causeways were constructed. Some of these old routes still survive and can be found, for example, near the Bridestones (Walk 1) and in the woods near Beck Hole (Walk 7). Egton (Drive 3) sits at the heart of a complex system of such routes, reflecting its old role as a major livestock market, first established in 1245. Other well-trodden ways were used by the fish hawkers, and a medieval route was established from Staithes, for instance.

Major road improvements came in the eighteenth century when turnpike trusts were established to build new roads and then charged travellers for the use of them. These form the basis for many modern road systems, and there are still memories of the days when the stage coach represented the ultimate in travel luxury. The Black Swan at Helmsley, for example, is an old coaching inn and stopping place for the 'Helmsley Flyer'. But the new roads had scarcely been completed before a new rival appeared — the railways.

The North Yorkshire Moors Railway, running from Pickering to Grosmont, is the best-known line in the region. Here, the great days of the steam locomotive live again and you might think, looking at the steam engines and the old restored stations, that the line has been brought back to the way it was when the first trains ran. Nothing of the sort! When the line was officially opened in 1836, no hiss of steam was heard; not a whistle tooted. Instead, there was the 'clip-clop' of hooves as horses pulled a stage coach with flanged wheels along the track. The engineer responsible for this line was the famous George Stephenson, and one of the features of the line was the 1500-foot-long (457-m) incline at Beck Hole where trucks were hauled up the slope by cable. You can see Incline Cottage from Walk 7. By 1847, however, the line was converted for steam, abandoning the old incline, and joined to the new main line from York to Scarborough.

KEY TO WALK MAPS

- - - - - -	Route of walk
▬▬▬	Main road
▬▬	Other road
- - - - - - - - -	Footpath
┝━━━┿━━━┥	Railway
P	Car Park
PC	Public convenience
i	Information centre
🚶🚶 🚶🚶	Direction of walk
♜	Castle
⅄	Camp site
⊼	Picnic site
⊟	Caravan site
▣	Telephone
⊕	Mountain rescue centre
✕	Mountain shelter
YH	Youth Hostel
◆	Monument
⊻	Viewpoint
†	Church
⛰ ⏶	Peak / hill, outcrop
♣ ♣	Wood
▤	Town / building

Passengers on the North Yorkshire Moors line enjoy the magnificent scenery — as did the passengers who travelled on the new line from Whitby to Scarborough in 1885. It was a late arrival on the railway scene — and was destined never to reach its centenary for it fell to the Beeching axe in 1965. But the line is not quite dead, for a good deal of the old trackbed is now a path, used by walkers, cyclists, and riders. The section from Ravenscar to Robin Hood's Bay is featured on Walk 8.

Transport across the moors is not, however, all firmly fixed on the ground. Military jets regularly practise, screaming by at low level while the early warning system at Fylingdales has long provided the area with one of its more bizarre monuments — the three great golf balls on the moor, now being replaced by a large pyramid.

THE BRIDESTONES

1¾ miles (2.8 km). Allow 1 hour. Easy.

This short, easy walk makes an ideal introduction to the North York Moors. It includes two of the typical elements of the scenery — heather moorland and wooded valley — and adds an extra ingredient, a set of bizarre-shaped rocks. Although it is a short walk, it offers great variety and runs through National Trust land.

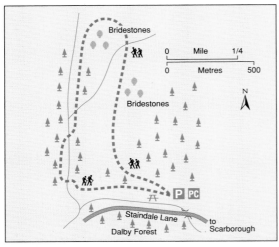

The walk begins at the Staindale Lane car park on the north side of Dalby Forest alongside the toll road. Grid Reference SE878902.

Cross the grassy picnic area and head for the National Trust sign. The path goes on through the trees, mainly oak, birch, and rowan. This area of deciduous woodland, virtually surrounded by conifer plantations, has been declared a Site of Special Scientific Interest (SSSI). Redstarts, blue tits, great tits, and sparrowhawks frequent the woods, while the red grouse feed on the moor; among the more exotic visitors to the region are merlin, hen harriers, and the attractive emperor moth.

Turn right by the large notice board to go through the stile to join the path through the main area of

(Below) The path dips downwards on a paved pannier or pitched way from the Bridestones (right).

woodland. Almost immediately, the path divides: turn left on the gentle uphill path overshadowed by oak and birch. Even when you cannot see the woodland birds, you can hear them all around you, from the harsh screeching of the jay to the hollow 'hoo-hooing' of the wood pigeon. Squirrels can be glimpsed scampering among the trees. The top of the hill is reached through an avenue of silver birch and here are the strange, weathered shapes of the Bridestones. The path comes out into an area of heather and coarse grass, with wide expanses of heather moorland spreading away into the distance. The path, covered in a layer of fine, soft sand, leads on to the stones themselves. Wind, rain, and ice have shaped and pitted the rock, which wears unevenly so that the rocks look like piles of massive plates; while one of the stones has been undercut so that it now balances on a slender pedastal, looking rather like a giant font.

The path runs along the lip of the valley — hence the original name of Brink Stones — and there is a view down the fern-covered slopes to the woods at the bottom. The path now dips downhill on a paved pannier or pitched way to the dark-green cleft where a little stream runs under the shadow of rowan and

birch. The route climbs up the opposite slope to the second group of rocks, one of which has been eroded to create a tunnel right through the middle. Turn left to follow the path that runs along a ridge between two deep valleys, dotted with rather stunted trees. To the left, the Bridestones stand out impressively against the skyline; to the right, the ferny slopes lead up to farmland on the plateau with wilder moorland beyond. This is quite a steep stony pathway that needs to be treated with a certain amount of caution. The steeper sections are again paved with stone blocks.

The path leads down to a footbridge over a little winding stream, that meanders through the meadows on the valley floor. Cross the bridge and follow the path round to the left by the stream. This is a very different environment from the moorland. In summer, wild flowers gleam through the tall grass — marsh marigold down by the stream, buttercups, clover, meadow saxifrage, and bugle in the meadow. Recross the little stream, go over the stile, and turn left to follow the path round the edge of the woodland. For this final part of the walk, oak and beech lean over the path to shade the way. Go over the stile by the farm gate to return to the picnic area and car park.

FARNDALE
3 miles (5 km). Allow 1½ hours. Easy.

This is an easy walk at the upper end of the beautiful valley of Farndale. A walk of contrasts, at first it follows a gentle river valley, but returns along the edge of the moorland with views over one of the loveliest and least-frequented dales.

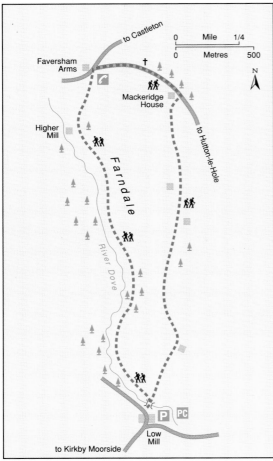

The walk begins at the Low Mill car park on a minor road through Farndale. To reach it, leave the A170 at Kirkby Moorside and head north through Gillamoor. Grid Reference SE 673952.

From the car park, go through the gate by the sign 'Public Path to Higher Mill' and follow the path downhill to the river. Cross the bridge and turn left to follow the river upstream. The character of the walk quickly establishes itself. To the left is the busy stream, stained brown by the peat of the moorland; to the right farmland spreading away in a patchwork of fields bounded by drystone walls that straggle up to the edge of the moor. In spring, this valley is a mass of daffodils, and local legend has it that this was the inspiration for Wordsworth's poem. The river is crossed by a weir over which the water cascades. Originally, this enabled some of the river water to be diverted into a leat to turn the wheels of the mill that gave Low Mill its name. Just beyond the weir is a willow-fringed pool, home to a small colony of mallard. This is a good firm footpath, bordered by fern with patches of oak and elder woodland.

The path rises on a bank above the stream, which sets off on an increasingly erratic course, winding and wriggling through the land, while the path continues on an altogether more direct route. It continues across rough meadowland and the view opens out on the right to the rim of the valley with its hard edge of rocky outcrops. It proceeds, via a succession of stiles, through fields speckled with daisies, clover, and thistle. The river is rejoined at a little area of woodland, and the path goes through a gate with two arrows; continue straight on. Note that in 1991 a proposal was put forward for rerouteing this part of the path. This section of the walk ends at Higher Mill. The three-storey stone grain mill has now been converted into housing, but it is still possible to see the watercourse behind the mill, where the water wheel once turned.

The path passes the mill on the broad farm track that leads to the group of buildings underneath the trees — do not cross the stile by the yellow arrow. The track is bounded on one side by a stone wall and on the other by a hedgerow with brambles and dog roses. Up ahead the valley divides round a hillock and there are extensive views out over the hills that surround this delightful dale. The track ends at the

Low Mill Post Office.

roadway by the Faversham Arms, a fine traditional inn with stone-flagged floor. Turn right up the roadway signposted to Hutton-le-Hole. On the left is the church built of massive sandstone blocks, with a simple whitewashed interior and barrel vaulted roof over the chancel. It was rebuilt in 1831 by Lord Faversham and a gallery added and, as the original sign explains, '...it contains sittings for 300 persons, the whole of which are thereby declared to be free and unappropriated for ever'. It is difficult to imagine where a congregation of 300 could be found in this remote valley. The church has been altered again since 1831.

The walk continues up the quiet lane, bordered by trees, including a magnificent copper beech, and climbs gently all the time, giving ever wider views over hills and moor. Just beyond Mackeridge House near the top of the hill, turn right by the Public Footpath sign to follow the path by the stone wall. Almost immediately, turn left to cross the wall by the stile and head towards the farm buildings. Continue straight on, following the sign for Footpath to Low Mills. At the corner of the stone walls, leave the broad farm track by the gateway and the disused stile and cross the field as indicated by the footpath sign. Cross the stone stile and go through the farmyard past the farmhouse; leave by the gate and head for the stile opposite. At the wooden stile, head diagonally across the field as indicated by the arrow, leaving the modern barns to the left, and head for the gate in the far right-hand corner of the field. Follow the path down by the hedge with its line of oak trees. At the corner of the field, turn through the gateway and continue along the bottom of the field to join the farm track. Go through the farmyard, turn right through the gate, and go downhill by the stone wall. Follow the shady stream, cross the stile and the brook, and head diagonally on the paved track following the line of telegraph poles towards the houses. At the bottom of the field, cross the bridge and return to the start.

(Below) One of the many stone stiles you will find in the area. (Bottom) The beautiful view over Farndale.

Walk 3
STAITHES

3 miles (5 km). Allow 2 hours. Moderate.

This walk combines a visit to one of the most attractive fishing villages on the north-east coast with a cliff-top walk and a country stroll across fields and through woodland. Be prepared for muddy and rather steep paths in the woods.

The walk begins in the car park above Staithes. To find it, turn north off the A174 and the car park is on the right. Grid Reference NZ 782185.

Turn right out of the car park and go down the hill to the harbour. The village first appears as a jumble of slate and pantile roofs, overlooked by sandstone cliffs, home to noisy colonies of wrangling gulls. At the heart of Staithes is a narrow, cobbled street, along which open entrances give glimpses of little yards crowded round with cottages. Eventually the street arrives at the harbour, once packed with fishing boats, sitting snugly in the shelter of the cliffs. Turn uphill along Church Street, following the Coast Path sign, past the mission church of St Peter the Fisherman. Everything has a nautical air, including one house with a figure-head over a shed. Continue straight on as the cobbled street becomes a footpath that leads to the cliff top. Looking back, there is a good view of the deep wooded cleft that ends at the village and the surrounding cliffs.

Near the top of the hill, turn left following the signpost 'Cleveland Way' up a narrow path between high banks. The path emerges by farm buildings and continues to follow a line between arable fields and the grassy slopes that lead down the cliff edge. The fields come to an end at an area of rough grassland dotted with gorse bushes, across which the path leads on to a stile near the cliff edge. From here, there are splendid views all around the coast, where shaley cliffs drop sheer to a pebble beach and rock-strewn shoreline. As the walk approaches Port Mulgrave, large sandstone blocks, neatly carved not by a master mason but by the weather, appear at the cliff top.

Port Mulgrave, originally called Rosedale Docks, was established in the 1850s to ship ironstone from the local quarries. It went out of use in 1916, and is now a beautiful and peaceful area in the care of the National Trust. Leave the path and continue along the road, which provides views of the now some-what crumbled remains of the piers that still provide cover for a few fishing boats. The road passes a row of cottages that started as a commu-nal lodging house for the ironstone miners. At the end of the ter-race, turn right on to the gravel path marked Public Foot-path. Go through the wooden gate in the direction indicated by the footpath sign. This is a pleasantly open section of the walk across green fields with wide views over to the moors — though rather blighted by a giant cement works. From the crest of the hill, head down to-wards the stile and continue along the edge of the field to the main road. Cross the road, turn right into the layby, and then left over the stile by the footpath sign

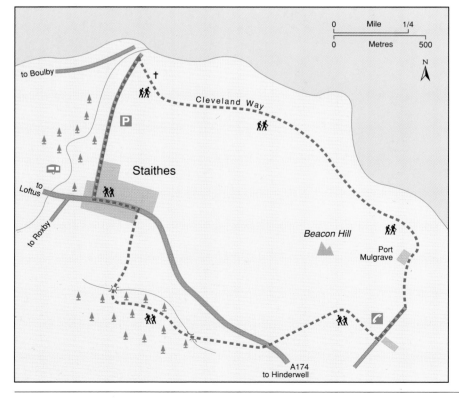

and head down to the wooded valley.

Head steeply downhill through an area of thorn bushes and trees to an area of dense woodland through which the path winds its way to a stream at the bottom. Cross the stream on the footbridge and follow the path round to the right — **not** in the direction shown by the yellow arrow. This little path is steep and can be slippery in wet weather. Cross the stile at the edge of the wood and turn right into the field. This is genuine meadow, bright with flowers including wild orchids. The path eventually comes downhill to a stile by a small

caravan park. Continue on across the stile, then turn right across the footbridge, and right again to the entrance to the caravan park. Take the footpath immediately to the left of the gate, cross the stile, and turn right into the woods. At the clearing, head straight uphill between two patches of woodland and continue on, leaving the farmhouse to the left.

Cross the stile, go over the farm track, cross the fence opposite, and continue straight on by the edge of the field to the stile by the garage. Cross the main road, turn left, then right down the Staithes road to return to the start.

(Above) Port Mulgrave. (Below) The view of Staithes from the cliff.

Walk 4

HAMBLETON FOREST AND THE RYE VALLEY

4 miles (6.4 km). Allow 2 hours. Moderate.

The head of the Rye Valley is peaceful and remote, surrounded by hills and moorland. Extensive conifer plantations have been added to the already extensive areas of broad-leaved woodland. The character of the walk is created by the change from green woodland to airy tracks along the fringes of the moor.

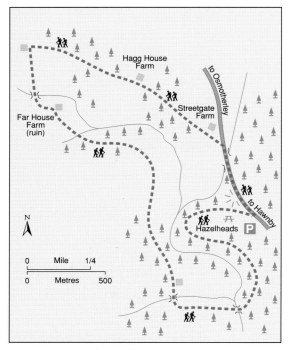

The walk begins at Hazelheads car park in a grassy clearing in the Hambleton Forest. This is on the minor road from Hawnby to Osmotherley some 2½ miles (4 km) from Hawnby. Grid Reference SE 530928.

From the car park, turn left down the road. At once the nature of the walk proclaims itself, with a view of woodland and, beyond that, a grand panorama of rounded hills. The road runs downhill to a stream that tumbles over a small waterfall and runs on down a narrow rocky valley. The road climbs back uphill to clear the woodland. Shortly after the cattle grid, turn left on to a public footpath towards Streetgate Farm, and continue on the green lane past the sturdy house with magnificent views out over the valley. The path runs across fields and into a green lane above birch and oak woodland that seems to be tumbling down the steep hillside. In parts this is used as a farm track and can be very muddy. Beyond the little wood, it emerges into a meadow bright with flowers that slopes away to a wooded valley and heather-covered hills. The path passes in front of Hagg House Farm, where farmhouse and barn are joined under a com-

The path near Hagg House Farm.

mon roof. Take the track to the right, above the open barn, and continue down the lane between stone walls. Here there are some of the best views of the rounded hills that surround the valley head. Continue on this lane to the next farm.

Go into the farmyard and turn left through the wooden gate and follow the path by the hedge downhill. The path is very indistinct in the long grass, but head downhill to the stream and turn left to follow the bank round to the footbridge. Cross the stream, turn right, and immediately left on to the broad path at the fringe of the moorland. Follow the track through the ruined buildings and turn left on to the track that runs between stone walls. Follow the wall round to the left and go through the wall heading for the prominent wooden stile in the row of trees opposite. Beyond the trees is the beginning of the open moor. Cross the little stream and follow the path through the trees at the edge of the moor, with the river as an accompaniment, rushing and tumbling below. The path goes on to a little stone barn. Take the path to the right up to the woodland and follow the wall and fence round to the gate. Take the narrow, but quite distinct, path through the rather dense woodland of birch and oak. Once out on the other side, the path climbs uphill by the wire fence, and there are views right over to the radio mast on Bilsdale Moor. The path goes past a ruined farm where only the outbuildings are in use.

Continue on across the farm track still following the line of the fence to a gate in the corner of the field. Go through the gate and continue downhill to the stream. Tall beech trees now join the more familiar oak and birch. Cross the stream at the ford and turn left to follow it downhill past the little ruined stone buildings. Go through the gate and continue on beside the stream to a gate with a yellow arrow. The path continues through an avenue of trees to another gate with a yellow arrow, and heads down to the stream. The path turns to the right and then left to a footbridge.

Once across the footbridge, continue straight on to the forestry plantation. The path curves uphill to meet a broad track. Turn left to take this track which winds through a typically dense array of conifers. At the edge of the wood, go through the gate and continue on the broad track to the next gate which opens out to the grassy picnic area and the start of the walk.

The ruins of Far House Farm (above), with stone walls and barns on the hillside (below).

Walk 5
ROSEBERRY TOPPING
5 miles (8 km). Allow 3 hours. Moderate.

The shapely hill of Roseberry Topping is the dominant landmark in the area. Walkers go from the attractive valley of Great Ayton to the hill and the moorland beyond it, and get a view of the monument to Great Ayton's most famous son, James Cook.

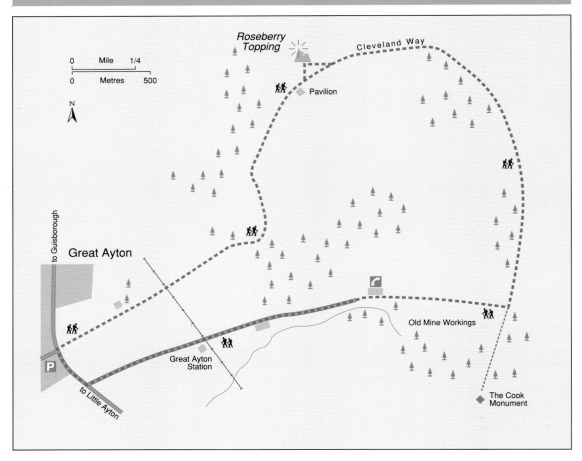

The walk begins near the green in Great Ayton where there is car parking at the edge of the green close by the Cook Museum (Grid reference NZ 562107). There is alternative parking at the foot of the track to the Cook Monument. Grid Reference NZ 592110.

Coming away from the village centre, follow the road round to the left, ignoring the turning to Little Ayton. Once round the corner, the walk gets underway. Go through the iron gate in the stone wall, signposted Public Footpath. Beyond it is an area of parkland with a little copse in the middle, dominated by a magnificent Copper Beech. The path goes right through the middle of the copse and continues on following the line of the hedge the shields the great house from view. At first, the walk is very gentle, a pleasant stroll beside arable fields and across the railway line, continuing as a broad track to an area of mixed woodland. Soon, however, it begins a steadily steepening climb.

At the end of the fields, cross the stile to follow the path into the woods. Beyond an iron gate, paths cross: turn slightly right, then diagonally uphill to the left through the trees. At the edge of the woods, do not cross the stile directly in front, but turn left and then right to go around the edge of the crops to head for the peak of Roseberry Topping. The path leads through fields bordered by hedges that, in summer, are bright with dog roses, then it steepens quite sharply as it reaches an area of coarse grassland with

gorse, fern, and foxglove. Here a charming little stone pavilion provides a resting point to admire the truly magnificent view.

The path now leads round the flank of Roseberry Topping, but the energetic can go up the steep path to the summit, half eaten away by quarrying. The grit stone faces drop sheer, in harsh contrast to the symmetry of the lower slopes. The main walk follows the line of the wire fence, which gives way to a recently rebuilt dry stone wall. The path dips down briefly before climbing steeply again along the side of the woods. Looking back, the quarried faces are now hidden from view and the hill is a perfect shapely cone.

At the top of the hill, turn right and go through a gate with the white acorn, an indication that this is now part of the National Trail, the Cleveland Way. Continue straight on following the stone wall along the edge of the woodland. To the left, heather moorland stretches away to the horizon. The path eventually reaches the roadway and the track up to the Cook Monument, a giant obelisk looking down over Great Ayton.

Turn right to walk down alongside the road. From here, there is yet another view of Roseberry Topping, now seen as rather an ungainly hump. The road winds down between banks of fern and gorse, with an area of spoil from old mine workings to the left. The moor is gradually left behind for a softer landscape, and dog roses replace gorse at the road's edge. It passes an attractive wooded valley with a small stream, and Great Ayton Station, now reduced to a single platform and a long way from the village. It was built in the days when the convenience of engineers was more important than that of the passengers. The village is approached down a tree-shaded lane. Follow the road round to the right, but notice a curiosity at the junction — a little cast-iron gents' lavatory tucked in beside a shed. At the main road, turn left to return to the start.

The pavilion, with Roseberry Topping behind (above), and the path through the woods (below).

Walk 6
URRA MOOR
5½ miles (9 km). Allow 3 hours. Moderate.

Urra Moor is the true North Yorkshire moorland, a high plateau, covered with heather, that spreads away to far horizons. Being at the edge of the moor, it provides walkers with superb views out over the plain to yet more distant hills. It is crossed by two longer routes, the Cleveland Way and the Lyke Wake Walk.

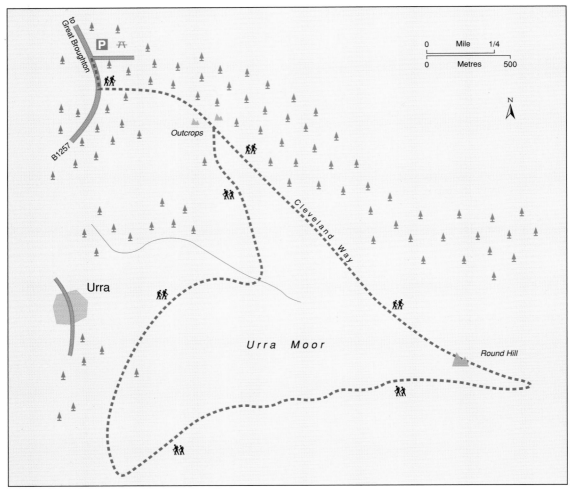

The walk begins from the large car park and viewpoint on the left of the road near the top of the hill leading up to Urra Moor. This is the B1257, 2 miles (just over 3 km) south of Great Broughton. Grid Reference NZ 572035.

Start by leaving the car park and turning left up the road, until a wooden gate on the left is reached beside a signpost for the Cleveland Way. The path follows the stone wall beside the forestry plantation, then heads straight on to the rocky outcrops at the top of the hill. As the path climbs, so the views open out first

to the rocky escarpment across the valley, then to a seemingly endless procession of flat-topped hills. The path divides and there is a choice between a direct scramble up the rocky gully or a longer but gentler route round to the left. The two paths reunite and the way continues through a gate marked with the acorn sign for a National Trail.

The route levels out to an altogether more gentle slope as the path leads on across the broad expanses of the moor. Sandstones show through the path. When these erode, they create a poor acidic soil, which supports heather and little else, while sphagnum moss grows in the boggy areas. It can seem a desolate area in winter but, in late summer when the heather is in bloom, it has a unique beauty. There is a special quality about the moors that seems to find a voice in the rather plaintive calls of lapwing and curlew.

The path climbs slowly and a steep-sided rocky valley comes into view to the left. A line of shooting butts serves as a reminder that the best-known inhabitant of the high moors is the red grouse. At the top of the moor is a cairn at a height of about 450 metres (1500 ft) above sea level. At a boundary stone, carved with the initials AM, turn right down the broad track. Where the track divides, continue straight on along the path which soon begins to zig-zag through areas of peat. It continues past a long line of substantial grouse butts, stone built and covered with heather. At the end of the line where the track divides, continue straight on downhill past the stone with the Newton Tower Estate plaque. Just before the land falls steeply away, there is a large notice board. Forty-five metres (50 yds) beyond it, turn right on to the narrow path through the heather which runs above the top of a deep gully.

The path now follows the edge of the escarpment, giving views down into the more fertile valley with its regularly spaced farms, each surrounded by neatly squared fields running up to the edge of the moor. The path follows the dry stone wall, and is very boggy in places. Follow the stone wall until its sweeps downhill, and continue on the path that hugs the rim of the valley. Large sandstone blocks outcrop on the edge, while the walk follows the line of an artificial bank and ditch. A gully bites deep into the hill and

the path follows it round, dips briefly down to a peaty stream trickling through the rocks, and climbs up again to continue following the edge. Down the slopes are spoil heaps, reminders of old ironstone mine workings. Now the heather is joined by dense clumps of bilberry.

Eventually the path widens to come out by dry stone walls that lead on to the gate with the acorn sign which you met on the way up. Turn left to return to the start.

The view across the plain towards Roseberry Topping (above), and the path across the moorland plateau (below).

Walk 7

MALLYAN SPOUT AND WADE'S CAUSEWAY

6½ miles (10 km). Allow 3½ hours. Difficult.

A waterfall tumbling to a rock-strewn river and a miraculously well-preserved Roman road are the star attractions of this walk, but it also includes paths with fine views over some of the best moorland scenery. The walk can be broken down into two shorter walks: one to visit the Roman road — this walk is about 4 miles (6.5 km); the other to Mallyan Spout which would also be a walk of about 4 miles (6.5 km).

The main walk begins from the broad parking area to the left of the road which is reached by taking the Hunt House road from Goathland, signposted for the Youth Hostel, and continuing down the road to the turning place where you turn and park. (Grid Reference SE 815989). For the Mallyan Spout short walk, park in Goathland village.

For the start of the main and Roman road walks, from Hunt House, walk back up the road towards Goathland. Turn left off the road after a quarter of a mile (400 m) on to the path through the bracken by the Public Footpath signpost. At the wire fence, where a signpost says 'Foss', do not turn left but continue straight on along the path by the side of the

fence, heading for the white house. Turn left on to the road and head downhill for the river. Those doing the shorter Roman road walk should continue straight on over the bridge and rejoin the main route half a mile (800 m) up the road by taking the left turn at Julian Park. For the full walk, turn right over the stile just before the bridge to join the footpath beside the river.

This path is something of a scramble among large boulders, as the valley becomes a more dramatic gorge with high rock faces showing among the trees. The river itself is a syrupy brown, stained by the moorland peat. It takes a tortuous, splashing route between rocks among which dippers wade. In general, walkers have to find their own best route among the rocks but, where the path divides just before the stone wall that crosses the route, the upper path is the easier. Crossing the wall by the stile brings a gentle woodland section, but this is short lived as the path goes uphill via a series of steps to the rocky pool where the waterfall of Mallyan Spout tumbles over moss-hung ledges. The path goes past the bottom of the falls, with a scramble over rocks near the water's edge. It emerges on a broad path, where walkers doing the short Mallyan Spout walk join the route. This walk has a different start: from Goathland village, take the path through the iron gate next to the Mallyan Spout hotel which comes down to this point. Join the main walk which continues to follow the river and is signposted to Beck Hole.

The stream through Scar Wood (left), and Wade's Causeway (below).

The path gradually climbs to the lip of the valley, with woodland to the left and fields to the right. It emerges to a more open section with wider views, then dips steeply downhill to the hamlet of Beck Hole. Here it briefly joins the old Stephenson railway line by Incline Cottage. Where the way diverges by a signpost, turn left following the blue arrow, marked Bridleway, to cross the river on a footbridge. Follow the path straight ahead up the steps and continue through the avenue of conifers. At the top, turn left by the signpost on to the narrow footpath through the woods. This is an old packhorse route with stone blocks set on the slopes. All the way this is a narrow path through dense woodland, with occasional clearings giving views across to Goathland. At the end of the woodland, cross over the stile, turn left at an angle to follow the hollow way up to the crest of the hill, then slightly right to follow the stone wall to the gate in the corner. Continue down the lane between stone walls. At the roadway, turn left.

Here the three routes meet. Walkers on the short Mallyan Spout walk follow the road round to the left to reach the bridge; walkers on the Roman road route, rejoin the walk at the corner. The main walk turns right down the lane between stone walls. This is a lovely high-level route with rough pasture on one side and moorland on the other, with wide views across the valley. After a mile (1.6 km), take the path in front of the farmhouse and go through the gate to a green lane; continue on the narrow grassy track signposted Bridleway. It is waymarked with blue arrows.

Turn right to cross the stream on the wooden footbridge, then left to follow the track up the hill signposted 'Footpath Roman Road'. At the top of the

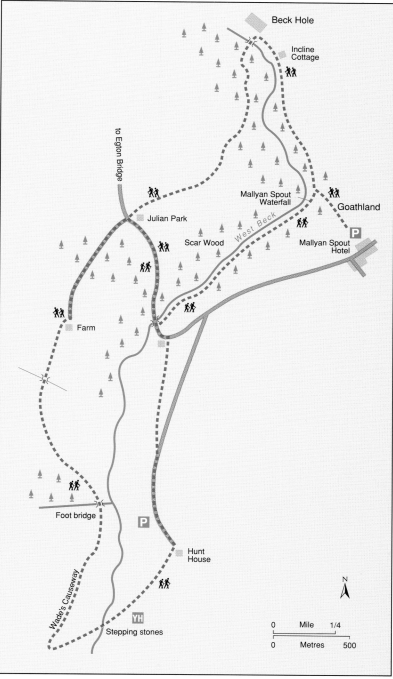

hill is the paved road itself, Wade's Causeway. Follow the road, cross the high stile, and, after 180 metres (200 yds), turn left by the notice board on to the path leading down off the moor. It is steep and stony and leads down to the river, which is crossed on stepping stones. Turn left to follow the track past the Youth Hostel and straight on to the metalled road to return to the start.

RAVENSCAR AND ROBIN HOOD'S BAY

The whole round trip is 8 miles (13 km) but it can be divided into two shorter walks: one based on Ravenscar of 6 miles (10 km); and one on Robin Hood's Bay of 3¾ miles (6 km). Allow 4 hours. Difficult.

The walk features the popular and picturesque resort of Robin Hood's Bay and the failed, but no less attractive, resort of Ravenscar. One part of the route follows a disused railway line and the remainder is a switchback path along the cliffs.

The walk begins at the roadside parking and car park close by the National Trust Coastal Centre at Ravenscar. Grid Reference NZ 979015. The car park for the Robin Hood's Bay short walk is at the top of the main street. Grid Reference NZ 952052.

The main walk begins by following the path from the road at Ravenscar past the National Trust Coastal Centre. At the end of the stone wall, where the path divides, turn left to join the broad track that passes under the bridge ahead. This is the trackbed of the old railway from Whitby to Scarborough. It runs between bushes of gorse, but opens out to give panoramic views over Robin Hood's Bay. It shortly arrives at an area of quarries with bright-red shale. These are old alum mines. The mineral was used as a mordant, for fixing colours when dyeing cloths. The ruined kilns come from a later brick works. To keep to a reasonably level route, the railway swings away from the sea in an extravagant curve, running with the ferns and rocky outcrops of the moorland on one side and green fields leading down to the sea on the other. As it moves inland, it reaches a very attractive section where farmhouses are dotted beneath the rocky rim of the moorland. Beyond the Browside Trekking Centre, the track goes into a deep cutting and an area of shady woodland, then emerges on to a high embankment giving views down on to the tops of trees. This is a common

railway practice, known as 'cut and fill': digging a cutting through a hill and using the spoil to build up an embankment over the next valley. It makes for great variety, for the sides of the cuttings are bright with flowers and the banks provide airy viewpoints.

The track passes under a three-arched skew bridge: look up to see the complex pattern of brick laying. Beyond that, steps lead down to the roadway where the three routes meet. Walkers on the short route from Ravenscar, turn right here and follow the road down to Boggle Hole to rejoin the main walk. Walkers from Robin Hood's Bay will have come up the same road and rejoin the main route.

Cross the road and continue up the steps to the platform which is all that remains of Fyling Hall station, though the station master's house still stands. Trees line the route to create a shady avenue. Cross the next road and continue on to the road by the houses at the outskirts of Robin Hood's Bay and turn right. At the T-junction on the B road, turn right to go past the car park which is the starting point for walkers on the shorter version of the walk. The cobbled street goes precipitously downhill to the sea.

At the slipway at the end of the street, turn right up the steps, go down the wooden steps towards the beach and then turn right again on the path marked 'Path to Clifftop'. From the top of the cliff, you have a fine view of the curving street running down to cliffs and the sea walls. Follow the path past a World War 2 defence post. At first, the path is over

(Left) The view across Robin Hood's Bay. (Below) Even dogs are catered for on this walk!

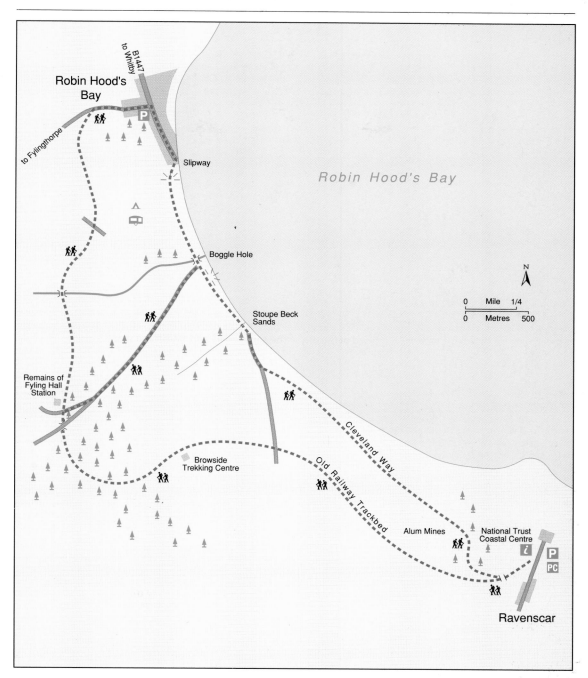

Robin Hood's Bay

B1447 to Whitby

to Fylingthorpe

P

Slipway

Robin Hood's Bay

Boggle Hole

Stoupe Beck Sands

N

| 0 | Mile | 1/4 |
| 0 | Metres | 500 |

Remains of Fyling Hall Station

Browside Trekking Centre

Cleveland Way

Old Railway Trackbed

Alum Mines

National Trust Coastal Centre

i P PC

Ravenscar

duckboards, but soon becomes a conventional, narrow clifftop path, part of the Cleveland Way. It drops steeply downhill to the peaceful inlet of Boggle Hole. Here one set of short-route walkers turn right to Fyling Hall, while the others rejoin the main walk.

Cross the stream on the footbridge and climb back to the clifftop, with superb views over the whole bay. The path soon drops down again to Stoupe Beck Sands. Back at the top, continue straight on along the road and, as the road bends round to the right, turn

left through a gap in the wall by a Cleveland Way signpost. This is a particularly attractive section of the walk on grassy banks that slope down to the cliffs. The path swings away from the sea. Turn left over the stile and join the broad track running between wire fences. Immediately beyond the small quarry, the path divides. Take the path to the right by the post with the acorn sign. It goes steeply uphill through an area of woodland. At the top of the hill, turn left, then left again to return to the start.

Drive 1
WHITBY, THE COAST, AND THE ESK VALLEY

42 miles (67 km). Allow 2 hours.

The drive runs along the coast from Whitby past the attractive village of Staithes, then crosses the open moor to the narrow, winding Esk valley. The town centre of Whitby becomes very crowded in summer but its old lanes, harbour, and the abbey on the cliffs where Dracula roamed in fiction are well worth visiting.

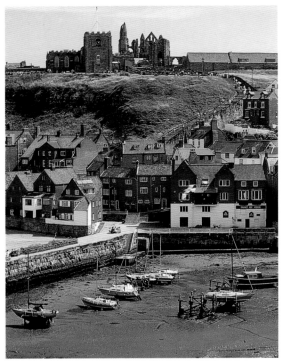

Begin the drive from the West Cliff car park on the outskirts of Whitby. Leave the car park and join the A174, turning right towards Loftus. The suburbs are soon left behind and the road runs right down to the sea at Sandsend. There is a pleasant little village clustered round the stream, as the road turns inland up a steep, winding hill. It continues on through Lythe through farming land with views over the moors to the left. A short diversion to the right leads to the car park above Staithes, the starting point for Walk 3; cars are not allowed down the steep main street of this picturesque fishing village. Return to the main road and turn right.

One mile (1.6 km) outside Staithes, by the cement works, turn right on to the unclassified road to Boulby. It twists along between stone cottages with views of rolling moorland and glimpses of the sea at Skinningrove. The broad beach with traditional cobles — wooden fishing boats — is overlooked by a steel works. From the harbour, the road swings left to go up the narrow valley to rejoin the A174. Turn left at the main road and then right at the traffic lights in Loftus on to the B1356 for Liverton.

At Liverton Mines, there are traditional single-storey miners' cottages. At the crossroads in Liverton, turn right on to a minor road that winds between high banks before diving and winding downhill into woodland and the little group of houses at Liverton.

The next village has many characterful old stone houses, and Moorsholm lives up to its name for a vista of moorland opens up ahead. At the A171, turn right and, after 1 mile (1.6 km), turn left on to the unclassified road for Castleton. The minor road arrives immediately at a great spread of open moorland, with rows of grouse butts and ancient burial mounds dotted over the landscape. Then the road descends to the lusher valley round Castleton. After crossing the railway and the river, turn left into Castleton, and left again in the village.

The road passes through Danby, where stone houses cluster round the green and sheep

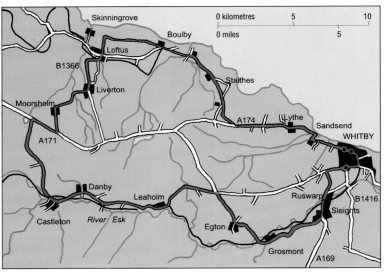

(Above) The handsome stone bridge at Leaholm. (Opposite) Tourists climb the steps from the harbour to Whitby Abbey. (Right) Duck Bridge, with the ruins of Danby Castle in the distance.

roam the village street. The National Park Information Centre is located here. The road continues, winding and twisting along the north bank of the Esk to Leaholm with its handsome stone bridge. At the T-junction by the river, turn left past the station and, at the top of the hill, turn right towards Whitby. At the A171, turn right and immediately right again towards Egton and Grosmont. The road runs at first through farmland but the moors are never far away. At Egton, a pretty village with houses set back behind a green, turn right at the junction and immediately left towards Grosmont.

The road leaves the uplands for a twisting route through a wooded valley and crosses the Esk at Grosmont on a fine eighteenth-century stone bridge. Immediately beyond is the North Yorkshire Moors Railway with its busy steam locomotives. There is a museum at the station. Turn left for Sleights and Whitby. This is a twisting switchback of a road. At the A169, turn left and, after 1 mile (1.6 km), turn right on to the B1410 for Ruswarp. Here there is boating on the Esk and an old mill. At the junction, turn left on to the B1416 and right at the roundabout for the centre of Whitby.

Drive 2
SCARBOROUGH, ROBIN HOOD'S BAY, AND TROUTSDALE

50 miles (80 km). Allow 2½ - 3 hours.

The first part of the Drive takes in the coastline between the two popular resorts of Scarborough and Robin Hood's Bay, then you turn inland through an area of extensive forests to Troutsdale before returning to the coast. Scarborough is a town with a long history as witnessed by the Roman signal station, the Norman castle, and the elegant buildings of the once-fashionable spa — now all mixed up with the popular seaside resort.

A convenient place to start the tour is the North Bay car park at Scarborough. Turn right on to the A165 heading north towards Scalby and Burniston. There are brief glimpses of the sea over to the right before the road turns inland for wooded hills. At Burniston, turn right on to the A171 towards Whitby. At Cloughton, as the main road turns sharply left, turn right on to an unclassified road that immediately passes the boundary of the North York Moors National Park. The road also brings more views of the coastline before swinging away through a rolling countryside of fields and woods. One mile (1.6 km)

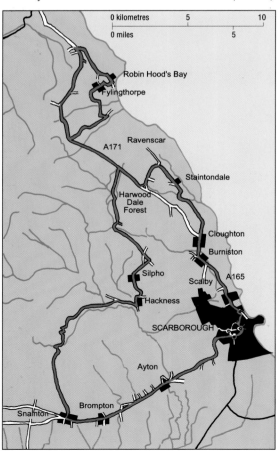

after Staintondale, turn left to return to the main road. The minor road that continues straight on leads eventually to Ravenscar and the start of Walk 8.

At the A171, turn right. The road runs through the middle of the extensive Harwood Dale Forest and emerges on the other side to an area of open moorland, which provides something of a roller-coaster, up-and-down ride. Turn right on to the minor road signposted to Fylingthorpe and Robin Hood's Bay. The road heads up to an area of very bare moorland from which there is a panoramic view over the wide sweep of Robin Hood's Bay. The road then goes steeply downhill to Fylingthorpe. At the T-junction, turn right for the car park above Robin Hood's Bay. This is one of the best-known beauty spots on the Yorkshire coast, with its houses seeming to tumble down the steep hillside towards the sea. The narrow streets become very crowded in summer.

At the turning point by the car park, turn and leave on the B1147. The clifftop ruins of Whitby Abbey soon come into view up ahead. At the A171, turn left back towards Scarborough, past the first Robin Hood's Bay turn, retracing part of the route. Five miles (8 km) beyond this turn, at the beginning of the Harwood Dale Forest, turn right on to the unclassified road. It goes through an area of dense conifer plantation, then comes out into the open to wind downhill to a little wooded valley before climbing up again to offer extensive views over the dale. The road dips down once again into a lush, green valley and then climbs again to a hilltop crowded with conifers. This is the start of the North Riding Forest Park through which it passes in a dead straight line. Go straight over at the cross roads, then take the next turning on the right, signposted to Silpho and Hackness.

In the area around Silpho, there are extensive views of the surrounding hills, many of them topped by woodland. Just before the road turns downhill again, there is a car park, a good place to pause and enjoy the scenery. The road now descends through a series of hairpin bends to Hackness. The little village is now dominated by the elegant Georgian Hall, but there was a nunnery here as early as the seventh century. Follow the road round to the right, passing the parkland and a lake shaded by copper beech. At the next junction, turn right and, after 1 mile (1.6 km),

The Iron Age earthworks at Troutsdale (above); a cobbled street in Robin Hood's Bay (right); and Chapel Farm on the edge of Fylingdales Moor (bottom).

turn left for Snainton and Troutsdale. The road crosses the River Derwent and makes its way through a valley dominated by trees, both mixed woodland and conifer plantations. The route becomes increasing tortuous as it climbs uphill through the woodland to a vantage point from which there is a view back along the whole length of the dale. The road then leaves the wood for an area of rough grassland before running through the farmland at the approach to Snainton.

At Snainton, turn left on to the A170 through Brompton, with the church in which William Wordsworth was married, and the two pleasant villages of West and East Ayton before reaching the outskirts of Scarborough.

Drive 3
PICKERING AND THE MOORS

41 miles (66 km). Allow 2 hours.

From the busy market town of Pickering, the Drive moves out to the great open spaces at the heart of the moors, visiting Goathland, one of the most attractive of the moorland villages, along the way.

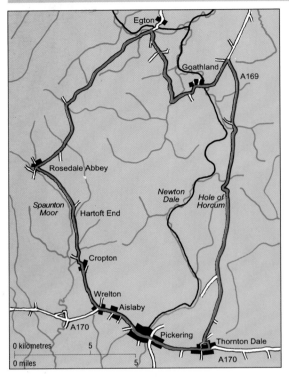

A convenient starting place is the Eastgate car park near the roundabout at the centre of Pickering. At the roundabout, take the A170 towards Kirkbymoorside. Immediately beyond Aislaby, turn right on to the minor road signposted to Cropton, Hartoft, and Rosedale Abbey, which passes through the little village of Wrelton. Turn right at the T-junction and follow the road as it bends round to the left. At first, this is a twisting country lane, running between banks that in summer are a mass of flowers. The road passes through the outskirts of Cropton and goes steeply downhill through woodland to enter the National Park with a view of the moors up ahead. Then the road disappears into the North Riding Forest Park and there are only occasional glimpses of the moorland through the trees.

There is a very grand inn at Hartoft End and the view opens up to Spaunton Moor. At Rosedale Abbey, a pretty spot with remains of a twelfth-century priory, turn right and then sharp right towards Egton. The road now climbs very steeply to the top of the moor and there are magnificent views over the valley. There is an area of completely open moorland,

marked only by the spoil of old ironstone mines and long lines of butts. Later the Fylingdales early warning station comes into view, though the famous 'giant golf balls' are due to be demolished by 1993 to be replaced by a new pyramid. Shooting butts continue to line the road.

The road comes down off the moor on a very steep hill towards Egton Bridge, once a major livestock market, now a quiet, attractive village. At the outskirts of the village, before the river is crossed, turn right towards Goathland; turn left at the top of the hill and continue following the road round to the right towards Goathland. There is a brief interlude of farmland before the road emerges on to rough moorland with Fylingdales prominent straight ahead. This is an attractive region which alternates heather moorland, pasture, and patches of woodland. The road swoops down to a little river and climbs up again to Goathland moor. At the T-junction, turn left for the village. Walk 7 starts near here. Goathland is a village of houses spread round wide greens where sheep graze, and it is a fine centre for exploring the moors. At the end of the village, the road swings round to the right by the station of the North Yorkshire Moors Railway. It crosses the lines and then climbs very steeply to the open moorland. On the approach to the main road, there are views right across the moors to the sea.

Turn right on the A169 towards Fylingdales. To the right is the deep ravine of Newton Dale with the steam railway snaking along the bottom of the valley. The road climbs through a hairpin bend to emerge above the great natural amphitheatre of the Hole of Horcum. After the moorland gives way to farmland, turn left by the inn on the minor road to Thornton Dale. The way is mainly open, though there is a brief dip into woodland before arriving at the main road and the village. There is much more to Thornton Dale than appears at first. It is a place of great charm, with little brooks running beside the village streets. Turn right on to the A170 to return to Pickering.

A locomotive of the North Yorkshire Moors Railway in full steam at Goathland (opposite); grouse butts on the moors (above); and the fine views over Rosedale Abbey (below).

Drive 4
HELMSLEY, THE HIGH MOORS, AND ROSEBERRY TOPPING

50 miles (80 km). Allow 2½ - 3 hours.

From the market town of Helmsley, dominated by its church and castle keep, the Drive soon climbs to the moors and continues right through to the northern edge of the National Park. It visits Great Ayton, with its memories of Captain Cook, then turns south again through some of the loveliest and most remote areas of the moors.

The Drive begins at the car park near the castle in Helmsley. Turn left on to the B1257. There is a steady climb through farmland. On the left is Rievaulx Abbey which is open to visitors, as is the terrace with its classical pavilions. The views open out to the left to the wooded valleys around Hawnby, and the road continues to climb steadily up to the Hambleton Forest. It then swoops down to the next valley of patchy woodland and scattered farmsteads. It passes through the little village of Chop Gate and the pretty hamlet of Seave Green nestling down in a hollow. The valley begins to narrow with woodland on either side and a steep hill rising up ahead. The road steadily climbs and

the scenery becomes ever more rugged with stony outcrops showing at the tops of the hills. At the very top there is a car park with superb views; this is the starting point for Walk 6.

The road winds down through conifer plantations to the valley below. This is a very different, much softer landscape. At Great Broughton, there is a reminder of one of the area's old industries — the Jet Miners Inn. At the Stokesley roundabout, take the A172 Middlesborough road and continue on the same road at the next roundabout. After half a mile (800 m), turn right on to the unclassified road to Great Ayton. The symmetrical cone of Roseberry Topping appears up

The drive starts at Helmsley (below), past Rievaulx Abbey (bottom), through Chop Gate (opposite top), with fine views of the moors (opposite centre), and down into the pretty village of Hutton-le-Hole (opposite bottom).

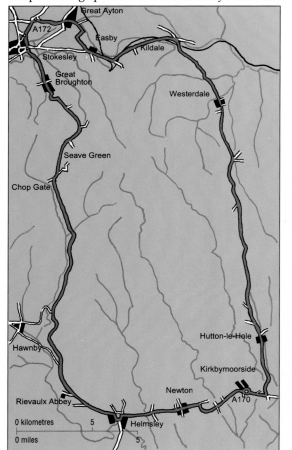